How to Improve Your Marriage without Talking About It

How to Save your Marriage and Heal or Repair an Unhappy Relationship

Amelia Farris

Amelia Farris

SOUTHSHORE
PUBLICATIONS & DISTRIBUTION

www.southshorepublications.com

ISBN- 978-1514100820

ISBN-10: 1514100827

Amelia Farris

CONTENTS

Amelia Farris

1. INTRODUCTION

We all wish we had a perfect marriage, but perfection is impossible. Especially when two different people with two different ideas of perfection are involved. The wonderful reality is that, even without this perfect life we have in our heads, you can feel really good in a marriage and you can feel extremely lucky to be with that special person you have chosen to spend the rest of your life with.

There are behaviors that you, just you, alone can do to improve your marriage for the both of you. There are things that you probably already do to improve your marriage without talking about it, maybe without even knowing it. In this short book, I am going to offer you some basic and unique strategies to hone these skills and master making your marriage into a place you really want to be.

This book is for when the honeymoon goggles wear off and real people come forward from the wedding bliss. You have shown each other little by little who you really are. You have to face that you are both human and not quite as perfect as you thought before the realities of marriage had sunk in.

The way your wife brakes too hard in the car may drive you nuts or the way he snores might keep you up for hours. The list goes on and on. The thing is, in a generally happy relationship these things won't bother you nearly as much.

You might have picked this book up, because you have lost some of the spark and the drive you one had in the partnership and you need to refocus a little to get life moving forward again. There is hope and I'm going to tell you how to fast track things towards the future you deserve.

It's necessary to be aware that you are dealing with another person who you can't necessarily control, nor would you want to, nor should you. Yet control does play a part in a marriage, and in life. I will discuss control later on in the book. The other person in your life has a whole set of rules and regulations that make them happy and function differently to you. Yet you will of course share some likes and dislikes. It is important that the other person is different. If you respect this, you can move forward in your marriage to wedded bliss with some completely nonverbal actions.

This book is about not having to say a word if you don't want to. This act comes easy for some and not so easy for others. This idea is going to put your actions in a higher realm of consciousness. You may get credit for what you do, or your partner may not even notice. Yet even without this credit, the reward of a vastly improved marriage will be more than enough trust me!

This book is about you being strong. These changes you are going to make are about you taking a responsibility for your actions and reaching out to your spouse so they feel content in their heart, and hopefully you will too.

If you are reading this then I know you are a caring thoughtful person and you deserve to be worshipped and taken care of by your spouse as you would like to. You deserve a well-balanced relationship that will keep you satisfied mind, body, and soul. You deserve this. You have already tapped into the kind soul that breeds a wonderful family unit, you deserve the best. Make sure you are getting it.

2. SOMETIMES SAYING NOTHING IS BEST

You will always hear that communication is key in making a marriage work, and for the most part, communication is very important. There comes a time though, where communicating just isn't the best option anymore. Especially if it has been tried and hasn't worked a few times before.

Sometimes in marriage we repeat ourselves and tell our partners things they already know to try and really get our point across. Sometimes we talk and say too much. Sometimes we like the sound of our own voice better than picking up the body language telling us that it is time to be quiet. These behaviors, although great for your own ego, are not always the best for the two of you.

At work you might be the type of person who finds out what has to be done, and you do it without having to be told. You are an adult, in control of yourself, and smart enough to accomplish what has to be done. Why should your marriage be any different than how you perform at work? You know what jobs have to be done around the house. There is always trash, laundry, cooking, dishes, and the house has to be clean and organized. So why can't your partner see that too? This kind of frustration is common in almost every relationship.

The house is not a place for ego battles. Both people involved should learn how to do everything in the house, so that if there is something that needs to be done, it should just be done without anyone ever having to talk about it. There is an exception when one person works, and the other's business is the house and cooking. It's a completely different story.

Whoever stays home and doesn't work, man or woman, their job is generally taking care of these things. This person will usually run the chores and errands and take care of the house like it's an efficient business by creating their own system. That being said, the other party needs to help when they can. They should never make the other person feel like they are the only ones doing the jobs around the house. This is up to them as well. They need to delegate if they need help. Remember a career person has a team of people at work helping them complete their job, and the house person has none, unless the family members contribute.

The house work is an easy place to do things before you are told to do them. Thus making it easy to help out and perform gestures of consideration and kindness for the other person without talking about it. This not only helps with not feeling pushed around, but it also shows respect for your significant other.

Not communicating and just doing things to help without talking about it works, but be aware to only do things that you know are okay to do. If you do something new and different the other person may actually get offended. Especially if they think you are doing it to make them look bad by essentially doing it yourself to make a point.

Sometimes though, you do have to take a chance and do things to help at the risk of them taking it the wrong way. This is a very effective way of making a change without talking about it. Just do something nice for them and help them out.

This kind of consideration and thoughtfulness for the other person really does go a long way and will be noticed. There is no need to tell them you have done anything or to go out of your way to gain recognition for it. If they don't mention it to you, just keep doing things and they will be picking up on the fact you're doing these nice things for them whether they are talking about it or not.

If you have an overemotional partner, as you probably know they just get emotional sometimes and you can't figure out why. You have to just leave them alone and let them get over it. This is another time when communication may not be the best answer.

It's tempting to feel a need to know what it is that is upsetting them. But you should remember that their emotions don't always have anything to do with you, and they're not always upset about something that you should have to feel responsible for. Emotional people sometimes just need to let it pass and they will be fine.

So make the odd, nice and helpful gesture and try and realize when you partner doesn't want to talk about things and just needs their space.

3. LOWER YOUR EXPECTATIONS

Many of us are guilty of having incredibly high expectations for our partners. A huge step you can take to help improve your marriage without talking about it is to throw all your expectations of what you want the other person to be like out of the window. Start loving them for exactly who they are.

This can be very hard to do because by doing this it can seem like you are giving up on everything you thought you wanted in a partner. All of the values and qualities you have been looking for for all of those years that you were dating are all idealistic and you can't really expect someone to meet every requirement.

Every person in this world does something eventually that you will not like. By making them feel overly bad about the little things they do wrong, or by harping on them for things they do that you think are inappropriate, you are pushing them away. Forget about all that. Take them as they are right now, without telling them. Don't say anything about your intentions, just start doing it today and you will start to notice a change very quickly.

You are going to do this by changing yourself. First you're going to make yourself better and just focus on you. You need to be the change that you wish there could be. You should try to live your life accomplishing something small every day.

It's futile to just sit around or keep having a go at them hoping your partner will suddenly change. This won't happen with no effort on your part. You are not going to wait for them, life is too short to wait for other people to make the first move. Even if you feel too proud to be the one putting in the work, it's going to be best for the both of you if you do.

You are just going to be the best you can be. In time your partner will see this difference and begin to react to this change in a positive way. It much easier for someone to react to a positive change rather than reacting to someone directly telling them to change.

It is difficult for some people to just let go of any resentment that they may have left over from previous arguments and make the first move on the step to recovery. But let me tell you, it's better than carrying on slipping down that road until you hit the point of no return.

It may feel like you are not doing much by initiating these subtle changes, but having you begin to release a little bit of pressure off of them may be just what the other person needs. This may give them the boost they need so that their mind has a chance to cool off and make sense of everything. No one can think straight and act rationally or fairly when they are stressed out. So try and cut them a bit more slack than usual and let things slide a bit more.

When you stop trying to force and control thing so much it is amazing how life unfolds in front of you in a much more interesting way. You have to pick and choose your main avenues of living. When you release the grip a little on life and allow certain things to happen and roll with them, life has a way of rewarding you along the way.

You cannot control everything. That is a fact. Don't worry if you get upset after you have allowed life to roll forward without you having as much control over it. I'm not saying completely let go, but try to find moments and times where you just don't have to have such a firm grip on everything that is going on.

Think about what part of your expectations you can put on your partner and what parts you shouldn't. It's important to be self-aware and know what you're doing to them. Usually when you criticize in your partner, it is really you that you need to work on because a lot of people will criticize based on these unrealistic expectations that I mentioned.

Maybe you think your spouse needs to lose weight. If this is the case volunteer to make a meal or two a week with healthier choices rather than just expecting them to make the change themselves just because you want them to. Cooking not only helps the other person with the mundane tasks of life, which relates back to what I was saying about nice gestures, but at the same to time it will help them lose weight without you having to tell them to do it. Its subtle ways around problems like this that are so simple but they will have a huge effect on you and your partner's happiness.

4. BASIC STEPS

In this chapter I'm going to go over some of the basic steps that you can take to really start getting your marriage on the road to recovery.

1. Make a Couple of Lists Just For Your Eyes

Without your partner knowing, take one month to make a list of all the places you believe you relationship needs improvement. This list is for you and you only, no guilt here just be honest. Now, make another list over the same month of the behavior you are doing that you notice gets a rise out of your partner. Then make a list of everything your partner does that you do not like. This may be things that make you feel insecure, unsatisfied, thing that make you feel angst, anxiety or any other type of negative emotion. Take a month to do this and don't worry or think about the list until the month is over. Pay attention to the little repetitive problems that occur as these recurring issues are what is most important. I will tell you soon what to do with the lists.

2. Consult the Internet for Solutions

If you have a very specific issue with your partner that is grating on you, look the solution up on the internet. Thankfully many of us go through the same things but in different ways. Just type in the words you're thinking of, for example, "how to get my spouse to stop leaving the towel on the floor," or "how can I get my spouse to stop spending and start saving", or basically anything else you can think of. You fill in the blank with the pressing problem and start reading. Let me make a note, though. Read a couple of solutions and let your intuition guide you as to what will work. Just because you need some solutions and there are some people they have worked for, that doesn't mean they will necessarily work for you and your partner. Be very diligent about analyzing the solution and make sure it applies to you.

3. Put Things in Perspective and be Flexible

If your partner is not happy with what you are saying or what's going on then try to back off a bit and don't press the issue too much. Learn to be considerate of the things that your partner does not like. Just stop behavior that's not flexible full stop. Two people in marriage are not in competition they are supposed to be in love, and work together. You can change your behavior right now if you really want to. Ask yourself if the things you do that annoy them are really worth doing. Do they mean that much to you that you will allow them to put such a strain on your relationship? If the answer is no, then just stop doing them and remember how insignificant they are compared to the health of your relationship.

4. Get More Sleep

Being tired is one of the biggest factors that will affect a person's level of self-control. If you want to master your own mind and your relationship, then the more sleep you get the better. Now let me say that there is a difference between laziness and getting enough sleep. Rest so your mind is sharp. Resting can just be making sure you sit down for ten minutes during the day and just close your eyes. Sleep is eight, ten or six hours. Whichever gives you the amount of energy to be fully alert and not waking up grumpy. When you are grouchy from not getting enough sleep, everyone can feel it, especially your partner.

Amelia Farris

5. INTERMEDIATE STEPS

Once you have implemented the basic steps, you can then move onto these tips and help you marriage heal even faster.

1. Let Your Spouse Think and Make Their Own Decisions

Let them think for themselves. Let them make their own decisions and have a good sense of self. This is so important. It's important for each person to have their personal time to themselves so they can think and sort things out in their own mind. Giving your spouse the opportunity to get away from it all, including you is a great way to make them happier in your relationship. Remember, the happier they are then the happier you will be.

You should protect each other's mind, body, and soul. Make them their own space or go away for a day and allow them to be alone and uninterrupted. You will respect them more if they have a strong sense of self and independence. A lot of people think that they wouldn't want this as it will create space between you. That space is so important in a relationship. When you get too close you will smother each other, and there's no quicker way to kill a flame than to smother it.

2. Don't Take Your Partner for Granted

Be appreciative that your partner is there for you. Let them know that you're thankful they are in your life. Some people just need that. They just need to know that you care. Don't be afraid to show you care. Don't go overbroad, just do a little something and go on to the next thing. Don't ever expect something in return, just tell them without needing something back from them. Give them a massage, or even buy them a massage. You don't have to do it all the time, but just every once in a while, make them feel really good. Care for them and say thank you when they do something nice for you.

3. Physical Contact without the Intention of Sex

Touch your spouse and get them used to you touching them without the intention of having sex. Allow your partner some time to get use to this. It is natural for some people to hold hands but it is not always natural for others. Be near each other and lean against each other. Just be close and have the physical contact without any intention of sex. Just hugging in public and feeling good together physically is key. Putting your hand on your spouse's back is a nice nonverbal comfort for example. Just try it without them saying anything, if they resist because it seems strange to them, don't worry, they will eventually learn to see it as being perfectly normal. Physical contact is key to emotional intimacy and is a hurdle that you have to get over if things have gone wrong in this department.

4. Agree with Your Spouse Even if You Don't

The hardest thing to do for some people, no matter whether it is a major issue or not, is to agree with their spouse when they do not believe what the other is saying. This is the number one essential thing to do for a successful partnership because how can you be a solid unit if you're always disagreeing? So right now if you truly love the person you're with, stop going against them. This does not mean you have to change what you believe in just show them some more support than usual. Be respectful of their opinions even if you do think they are wrong. Step in stride with what they believe in because you will boost their confidence and they will appreciate you for doing it. This is especially important in public, as disagreements in front of other people will lead to doubt and resentment.

6. THE ELEMENT OF CONTROL

Many partnerships have control issues. Both sexes can ego stroke and want to control their partner. If this is you, then quietly identify your need to control and learn where to control and where not to. There is helping someone get better if they have a hard time controlling themselves, but downright control because of your own emotional problems is not appropriate in any situation, least of all your marriage.

So let's take a look at this because it is complicated. Your spouse could do something that annoys you and you don't like it. In response, you may try to control them to make them stop. What are you achieving by doing this? You're not stopping them from wanting to do it or figuring out why they are doing it, you're just using your power over them and their feelings for you against them.

No one needs to be controlled completely. If you control someone you take away their ability to take care of themselves, and really in the end, life will be that much harder on you for doing this. Mainly because your partner will resent you so much as they will be able to tell exactly what you're doing.

The only person you can control is yourself. You can control your eating, your exercise, your cleanliness, and your own mouth. That is enough control. You can control your kids to a point, but you want kids that become self-sufficient healthy adults that know how to survive in this world at a good economic level. You don't want them to have emotional problems from too much control, so learn to lay off if you are one of those types of people. No one can control everything.

If you need to control then go be a director, or manager in a business. Utilize your need to control in a positive way and not in a negative way with another person in your family. No one has a one hundred percent control in any situation or over any other person. When you realize this and learn to accept it your life becomes a lot easier and less stressful.

So a big part of improving your marriage without saying a word is to quietly identify your own behavior. Look at how you try to control your partner. You may control them by manipulating their emotions. You may want them to do things a certain way and yell at them if they don't do things your way. Instead, let them do things their own way and you do your things your own way. It may seem impossible for you to grasp this right off the bat, but when you release some of your control over your partner's life, things will eventually get a whole lot better as they will feel more free and happy in themselves.

The idea of the two of you together is that you are individuals first that can take care of yourselves. You have come together in love to help and support each other because life is better with a friend with someone to support us. It's a great feeling to support someone else and help them through life, but too much guidance and you will smother them.

Life is no fun if you're just being selfish all of the time. You must learn how to think outside of yourself and allow the universe to flow freely without your need to control every little thing.

7. TALKERS VS. NON-TALKERS

There are both men and women that like to talk and those who don't. Many times talkers marry non talkers, because the balance helps keep the marriage going. It is also excellent to marry someone different than yourself, because you can be amazed at what someone else can do and what you can learn from them.

It is very important for talkers to be very sensitive to non-talkers and know when to be quiet or leave an issue alone. Talkers like to analyze, get into details, and gossip a little. Non talkers are straight forward. They generally don't read into things the way talkers do, nor do they want to. Talkers and non-talkers have different tolerance levels for different things. It is important as either a talker or non-talker to understand and respect the make-up of the other.

A talker should always be respectful of a non-talker and a non-talker needs to sometimes just listen to the talker just so they can get whatever is bothering them of their chest without too many comments or negativity.

These things can be done without a word just by listening. This is the single most important way to improve your marriage without saying a word. By simply listening to what the other person is saying and properly taking it in without dismissing it when you don't agree.

Just because someone does not talk doesn't mean they don't know what to say. Just because someone talks all the time does not mean they know everything. Be aware of these facts and be sensitive to these areas. Talkers need to walk away and talk out of earshot of the non-talkers. Give non-talkers time to think, peace, and quiet. If you are a talker sometimes you need to just be quiet!

There is a time to talk and there are people who talkers can talk to who also love to talk and listen. If your spouse likes to talk a little but not as much as you do, realize that right now and change your behavior and talking habits. Make your point and get going. You do not have to be perfect and you'll need to run your mouth a little, but keep it under control and watch the behavior of your partner for when enough is enough. Everyone can instinctually tell when someone just is not listening anymore if you are aware.

Talking and communicating is a wonderful thing but it can waste a lot of time and be pointless if the other person doesn't want to hear it. So keep the talking to minimum if you're with someone like this. If you want to do wasteful talking with someone find someone who has the time to do that and do a little with them, but keep your spouse out of it.

Amelia Farris

8. LIFE WITH AN IMPROVED MARRIAGE

Let us look an example of a couple who improved their marriage without talking about it. It started with Jason the husband who realized after some time that his wife was taking him for granted because he stayed home and she went to work. She began to treat him less like a man and more like a servant and he did not appreciate the feeling. So he decided two things, he was going to search for a book to help him and he also decided quietly to make some changes himself at home so she would stop looking at him as a push over and started seeing him more a man.

Slowly but surely she responds to his change in attitude and behavior. Before long, the two of them find a really great deal on an extra-large king size bed that will move very little so both parties can get an excellent night's sleep.

Jason gets up early in the morning and does his exercises and prepares fruit smoothies with almond milk for the wife and packs her a healthy lunch sometimes and sometimes she goes out to lunch. They are both committed to being healthy for the other but don't deny themselves things they want in food. This saves money and keeps her healthy and happy. She completes one thing in the house three times a week to help out her husband. She really doesn't have to but it takes the full burden off of him a little. She also does the dishes at night as he is the one who cooks the meals.

They both stopped overspending and buying unnecessary things so they can start saving for their retirement. They make a pact to both have a savings account and only do entertainment every other week like going out or going to a concert so they can start paying down their debt and become more financially secure. They make a pact together, which did require speaking about it, but they were totally open and unbiased to the other's needs. They both pared down to the bare essentials but were respectful to one another for the little luxuries the other needed.

Sounds good right? Well follow the tips in this book and it is entirely possible to make little changes like this for yourself and your partner.

9. CONCLUSION

So we have explored many examples and methods, but the most important are the ones that apply directly to your relationship. Your relationship is unique. Please take the time and write those lists. If you have already done it and it hasn't been a month. I'm sure you can think of some things but not all of them, just wait the month out. Okay, so with the list the first thing you are going to do without a word is see what parts of your own behavior you can change. You can only realistically change yourself.

Do what people have known for years stop caring so much about the little things. Stop caring so much about being right. Look at the bigger picture. Form a united front with your spouse and start supporting each other every step of the way. Don't be too corny but just support each other.

Like I said, change any behavior of your own that is not making sense for the relationship or may be causing problems with your partner. It is time to grow up and stop being teenagers. Now you of course want to be realistic and if there is behavior you can't live without or it will harm you by letting go then don't. But be totally honest with yourself, do you really need to keep doing that thing that your partner is offended by or whatever it is?

With the repetitive issues on the other lists, you should to research them and see if there is anything you are going to be able to do without having to discuss it. The reason you want to clear all these little problems up is that you want to have a clean slate to move to another level in your relationship.

You want feel loved, and satisfied. There should always be warmth and love and caring somehow. I know there are people that are not the most affectionate but then even the small gestures will count for more with these types of people.

Once you have made as many changes on your own as you can, things should be much better between you both. Then the big test will come. Your spouse will already have noticed a change of some sort. Whatever you do don't let on that this was all a plan, just try to change things without saying anything and divert their attention so they don't become suspicious. So once you have done your work, in a calm and non-emotional way try to approach your spouse about helping them do the same thing as you have done.

Back off immediately if the person feels threatened in any way and just say you'll get back to them. Let them digest any new information they are getting from you. Just keep up your work don't get discouraged and have faith. Just keep exercising, eating well, and don't lose hope. You become the best you can and if your partner does not want to change then you may have to make the hardest decision to find a new one. I hope they will take this journey with us and want to be in a wonderful relationship with you.

Amelia Farris

10. FINAL THOUGHTS

Well I think that about overs it for this book!

If you want to stay up to date with my regular free book promotions and to also find out about my future releases you can sign up to my mailing list at -
www.southshorepublications.com/ameliafarris

If you would also consider taking the time to leave me an honest review on this book on Amazon I would be extremely appreciative of your feedback.

You can find all of my other books, full of essential advice for women, by simply searching for "Amelia Farris" on Amazon.

Thanks for reading and I hopefully speak to you all in the next book!

Amelia Farris

Made in the USA
Monee, IL
29 June 2022

98783189R00022